On the Job

Photographer

Place Value

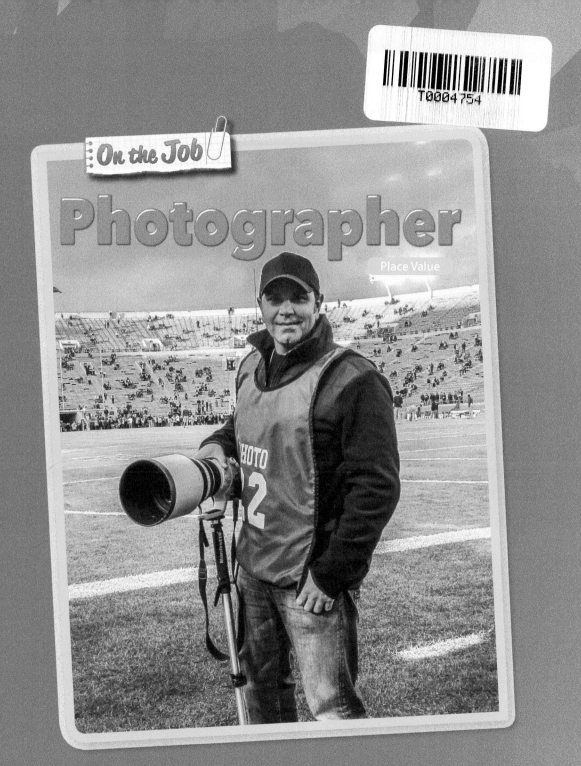

Kristy Stark, M.A.Ed.

Consultants

John Mattera
John Mattera Photography

Lorrie McConnell, M.A.
Professional Development Specialist TK–12
Moreno Valley USD, CA

Publishing Credits

Rachelle Cracchiolo, M.S.Ed., *Publisher*
Conni Medina, M.A.Ed., *Managing Editor*
Dona Herweck Rice, *Series Developer*
Emily R. Smith, M.A.Ed., *Series Developer*
Diana Kenney, M.A.Ed., NBCT, *Project Manager*
June Kikuchi, *Content Director*
Stacy Monsman, M.A., *Editor*
Michelle Jovin, M.A., *Assistant Editor*
Fabiola Sepulveda, *Graphic Designer*

Image Credits: front cover, pp.1, 8, 12 courtesy John Mattera; back cover, pp.2–3, 10, 11 (top), 13 (both), 15, 17 (both), 18–19, 22, 24, 26, 29 John Mattera; p.5 Jeff Loftin; p.11 (bottom) Caden Correll; pp.19 (bottom), 23, 25 Maria Mattera; p.21 Nicole Galasso; all other images iStock and/or Shutterstock.

Library of Congress Cataloging-in-Publication Data

Names: Stark, Kristy, author.
Title: Photographer / Kristy Stark.
Description: Huntington Beach, CA : Teacher Created Materials, [2018] |
  Series: On the job | Audience: K to grade 3. | Includes index. |
  Identifiers: LCCN 2017049046 (print) | LCCN 2017053324 (ebook) | ISBN
  9781480759916 (eBook) | ISBN 9781425857417 (pbk.)
Subjects: LCSH: Photography--Juvenile literature. | Photographers--Juvenile
  literature.
Classification: LCC TR149 (ebook) | LCC TR149 .S6844 2018 (print) | DDC
  770.23--dc23
LC record available at https://lccn.loc.gov/2017049046

Teacher Created Materials

5301 Oceanus Drive
Huntington Beach, CA 92649-1030
http://www.tcmpub.com

ISBN 978-1-4258-5741-7

Table of Contents

Meet a Photographer

Have you thought about what you want to be when you grow up? Think about the things you are good at doing. Think about the types of things that you like to do, too.

Maybe you like to **capture** memories. You can do this by taking photos. Someone who is good at taking photos can work as a photographer.

Meet John Mattera (muh-TAIR-uh). He is a photographer. John loves to take photos. He is very good at it, too. People pay him for his photos. His photos help people **recall** special events.

John Mattera

Photo Shoots

John takes photos at a lot of events. The events are special. People do not want to forget them. So, they **hire** photographers like John.

Some people ask John to take photos at their weddings. Or, they may want him at birthday parties. John takes photos of students **graduating** from school, too. These are all times people do not want to forget.

Students graduate from high school.

A bride and groom pose for photos on their wedding day.

LET'S EXPLORE MATH

Imagine that John takes photos at a wedding. John counts 20 people.

1. Describe how you can show 20 using only ones blocks.

ones block

2. Describe how you can use only tens blocks to show 20.

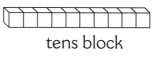

tens block

John takes photos at sporting events, too. He takes photos of his favorite teams. Then, he sells the photos. Some of his photos are used in news stories.

Sometimes, John takes photos that do not have people in them. Instead, he takes photos that show trees and flowers. Or, he may show other things in nature. These are called landscape photos.

John works at a football game.

John took this ocean landscape photo.

Imagine that John takes 100 landscape photos. Which of these models shows 100? How can you make the other two models show 100?

A.   B.   C.

The Necessary Tools

When John goes to photo shoots, he takes his **equipment** with him. He has a bag that holds all of his items. He packs the bag with tools he needs for the day.

The tools John brings **vary** based on the type of photo shoot. For all photo shoots, he needs his camera. He needs some memory cards, too. These cards are small discs that save the photos John takes.

John needs the most memory cards for weddings. He takes more photos at weddings than at any other type of photo shoot.

John's equipment

memory card in John's camera

X008

John uses memory cards to save photos. Imagine that each memory card holds 100 photos.

1. John reviews photos in groups of 10. How many groups of 10 can fit on one memory card?

2. John fills 6 memory cards. How many photos did he take?

3. John reviews 30 groups of 10 photos. How many photos does he review? How many memory cards do the photos fill?

11

In John's bag, he has many camera lenses. These lenses connect to the camera. A standard lens can be used for many types of photos. But John can change the lens when he needs to. The type of lens that John needs depends on the type of photo he is taking.

John needs a special lens for taking photos at sporting events. It is called a telephoto lens. This lens can be very big. It can cost a lot of money, too. But this lens can take photos from far away. John does not need to be close to the action to get great photos.

John takes photos at a football game using his telephoto lens.

telephoto lens on a camera

camera lenses

13

John uses a wide-angle lens for large scenes. This lens can capture big areas. John uses this lens for his landscape photos. He uses it to take photos of tall things, such as buildings and trees, too.

A macro lens takes photos of small things. These photos show a lot of details. John uses this lens when he takes photos of a bride and groom's rings. This lens can be used to show beads on a bride's dress, too.

John used a macro lens to take these close-up photos.

John took this landscape photo with a wide-angle lens.

At the Photo Shoot

Once John is packed, he goes to the photo shoot location. This is where the event will take place or where the **client** wants him to go. Once there, it is time to start taking photos. First, he finds places with the type of lighting he needs. John likes to use soft lighting in many of his photos. He thinks it is best for making his photos look great.

Next, John tries to make the scene look nice. But he does not want the scene to **distract** from the people in the photos. It is John's job to make everything look perfect.

poor lighting

good lighting

John used a slow shutter speed to take a photo of fireworks.

John must think quickly while he takes photos so he can catch special moments. John keeps his camera ready so he does not miss a thing.

John also checks his shutter speed. The shutter is the part of the camera that lets light in. John likes to use a fast shutter when he takes photos of things that move fast. He uses a fast shutter speed at sporting events.

A slow shutter speed is used to show **motion** in a photo. John uses this speed for photos of fireworks. It is John's job to know the best shutter speed for each photo.

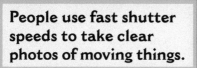

People use fast shutter speeds to take clear photos of moving things.

John takes lots of photos at each event. On some days, he needs help. One person cannot take thousands of photos at a wedding. So, he hires one or two other photographers to help him.

John may use two or more cameras with different types of lenses at one event. He does this so he does not have to stop to change the lens. John wants to take as many photos as he can. He wants his clients to have a lot of choices.

LET'S EXPLORE MATH

Imagine that John hires two photographers, Kyra and Victor, to help him.

1. John takes 50 groups of 10 photos. How many photos does he take?

2. Kyra takes 200 more photos than John. How many photos does she take?

3. Victor takes 40 groups of 10 photos. How many fewer photos than John does he take?

John takes photos at a wedding.

After the Photo Shoot

Once a photo shoot is done, you may think John's work is done, too. But much of his work is just starting. After the event, he looks at all of the photos. For some events, this may take hours!

John deletes any photos that are blurry. He picks photos that he thinks his clients will want to see. Then, he edits those photos. He may make colors look brighter. Or, he may take out spots or **imperfections** in the photos.

John edits photos on his computer.

John chooses the best images to show his clients.

After John is done editing photos, he shows them to his clients. His clients choose the ones they want to buy. They can get **digital** copies of the photos. Or, John can order prints of them.

Some clients want John to make photo albums for them. Making an album can take many more weeks. John chooses and edits many photos. It is a lot of work. But albums help his clients recall their special days.

John made this photo album for a bride and groom.

John edits his clients' photos to make them look their best.

Being a Photographer

Do you want to do what John does? If you like to take photos, this may be the perfect job for you. It is a good job to have if you like working with people. You get to meet people and help them remember great days through photos.

If you want to have this job, you can start now. Ask an adult whether you can use his or her camera. Take photos of things and people around you. With practice, you can learn how to catch special moments in photos.

A family takes photos together.

Problem Solving

Imagine that John is making photo albums. There are 10 photos on each page and 10 pages in each book.

1. John has 400 sports photos. How many photo albums does he fill?

2. John takes 900 photos at a wedding. How many pages does he fill?

3. After a birthday party shoot, John prepares 5 pages of photos. How many photos is this? Is it enough for a full photo album? How do you know?

4. A client who graduated orders 3 full photo albums. How many pages and photos is this altogether?

Glossary

capture—record something in a film or photo

client—someone who pays a person to do something

digital—files that can be viewed on a computer, tablet, or smartphone

distract—take attention away from something

equipment—tools or supplies that someone needs to do something

graduating—moving from one level of school to another level

hire—pay someone to do a job

imperfections—bad parts or flaws

motion—the act of moving

recall—to remember

vary—change

Index

Answer Key

Let's Explore Math

page 7:

1. Descriptions will vary but should include using 20 ones blocks.

2. Descriptions will vary but should include using 2 tens blocks.

page 9:

A. Image does not show 100; There needs to be 100 ones blocks, so 99 ones blocks must be added to the image.

B. Image does not show 100; there needs to be 10 tens blocks, so 9 tens blocks must be added to the image.

C. Image shows 100.

page 11:

1. 10 groups of 10

2. 600 photos

3. 300 photos; 3 full memory cards

page 20:

1. 500 photos

2. 700 photos

3. 100 fewer photos than John; Victor takes 400 photos, and $500 - 400 = 100$.

Problem Solving

1. 4 photo albums

2. 90 pages

3. 50 photos; It is not enough for a full photo album because full photo albums have 10 pages and 100 photos.

4. 30 pages; 300 photos